For He Will Order His Angels to Protect You Wherever You Go – Psalms 91:11

"For he shall give his angels charge over thee, to keep thee in all thy ways."
Psalms 91:11 King James Version (KJV)

My Journal

My Journal

For He Will Order His Angels to Protect You Wherever You Go - Psalm 91:11
Bible Verse Notebook/Journal with 110 Lined Pages (8.5 x 11)
Copyright 2016 My Journal, Don Cummings
(My Inspirational Journal) (Volume Three)
All Rights Reserved.
ISBN-13: 978-1539882527
ISBN-10: 1539882527

His angels will protect you.

My Journal

His angels will protect you.

My Journal

My Journal

His angels will protect you.

My Journal

His angels will protect you.

My Journal

His angels will protect you.

My Journal

His angels will protect you.

My Journal

His angels will protect you.

My Journal

My Journal

His angels will protect you.

My Journal

My Journal

His angels will protect you.

His angels will protect you.

My Journal

His angels will protect you.

My Journal

My Journal

His angels will protect you.

My Journal

His angels will protect you.

My Journal

His angels will protect you.

My Journal

His angels will protect you.

My Journal

His angels will protect you.

My Journal

His angels will protect you.

My Journal

My Journal

His angels will protect you.

My Journal

His angels will protect you.

My Journal

His angels will protect you.

My Journal

His angels will protect you.

My Journal

My Journal

His angels will protect you.

My Journal

My Journal

His angels will protect you.

My Journal

My Journal

His angels will protect you.

My Journal

My Journal

His angels will protect you.

My Journal

His angels will protect you.

My Journal

His angels will protect you.

His angels will protect you.

My Journal

His angels will protect you.

My Journal

My Journal

His angels will protect you.

My Journal

His angels will protect you.

My Journal

His angels will protect you.

My Journal

His angels will protect you.

My Journal

His angels will protect you.

My Journal

His angels will protect you.

My Journal

His angels will protect you.

My Journal

His angels will protect you.

His angels will protect you.

My Journal

His angels will protect you.

My Journal

His angels will protect you.

My Journal

His angels will protect you.

My Journal

His angels will protect you.

My Journal

His angels will protect you.

My Journal

His angels will protect you.

My Journal

His angels will protect you.

My Journal

His angels will protect you.

My Journal

His angels will protect you.

My Journal

His angels will protect you.

My Journal

His angels will protect you.

My Journal

His angels will protect you.

My Journal

His angels will protect you.

My Journal

His angels will protect you.

My Journal

His angels will protect you.

My Journal

His angels will protect you.

My Journal

His angels will protect you.

My Journal

His angels will protect you.

My Journal

His angels will protect you.

My Journal

His angels will protect you.

My Journal

Made in the USA
Middletown, DE
03 December 2016